LIVEWIRE
REAL LIVES

Leonardo DiCaprio

Julia Holt

Published in association with The Basic Skills Agency

Hodder & Stoughton

A MEMBER OF THE HODDER HEADLINE GROUP

Acknowledgements

Cover photo: Colin Mason.

*Photos: pp. 4, 10, 26 Rex Features; pp. 13, 17 The Ronald Grant Archive;
p. 19 photo Merrick Morton, the Kobal Collection; p. 23 20th Century Fox.*

Orders: please contact Bookpoint Ltd, 39 Milton Park, Abingdon, Oxon OX14 4TD. Telephone: (44)
01235 400414, Fax: (44) 01235 400454. Lines are open from 9.00–6.00, Monday to Saturday, with a
24 hour message answering service. Email address: orders@bookpoint.co.uk

British Library Cataloguing in Publication Data
A catalogue record for this title is available from The British Library

ISBN 0 340 74729 3

First published 1999
Impression number   10 9 8 7 6 5 4 3 2
Year   2004 2003 2002 2001 2000 1999

Cover photo from London Features International.
Typeset by Fakenham Photosetting Ltd, Fakenham, Norfolk.
Printed in Great Britain for Hodder & Stoughton Educational, a division of Hodder Headline Plc, 338
Euston Road, London NW1 3BH by Redwood Books, Trowbridge, Wiltshire.

Contents

1 Early Days

There is a small town
in the south of Italy,
10 miles from Naples.
900 of the people in that town
are called Di Caprio.
A lot of them have blonde hair
and blue eyes.

Leonardo DiCaprio's
great grandfather
came from that town.
He went to the USA in 1891.

The people in the town
are waiting for Leo
to come back
to his Italian roots.

Irmelin and George DiCaprio
went on holiday to Italy in 1974
from their home in America.
Irmelin felt her unborn son kick
when she was looking at a painting
by Leonardo Da Vinci.

George said it was a sign.
So when their son was born
on 11 November,
they called him Leonardo.

Leo's parents split up
before he could talk.
But they never divorced.
They shared the job
of bringing up their son.

Leo says he had a happy childhood.
He lived with his Mum
but he saw his Dad
almost every day.

He enjoyed the feeling
of being an only child.
But he does have
an older stepbrother, called Adam.

Leo with his mother.

Leo and his Mum
lived in a bungalow
at the end of an alley.

The area was called
the Hollywood Slums.
For four years, Leo walked to school
past graffiti and bullet holes.

Leo messed about at school.
He played the joker
because he wanted to be popular.
He said:
'School, I never truly
got the knack of it.'

Leo's hippy parents
tried hard to give him a good life.

People often mistook their little boy
for a girl,
because he had long blonde hair.

His Dad made hippy comics
in his garage
and Leo met many of the rock stars
and comic-book artists of the time.

2 Rejection

Money was always tight
for the family.
Leo even stole bubble gum
from the local shop

He saw acting as a way of
getting some money quickly.

Leo tried to get work on TV
when he was five.
But he was rejected
for a part in *Romper Room*
because he was too wild.

It was 11 years
before he landed
his first big screen part.

Meanwhile his stepbrother, Adam,
was making a lot of money
by acting in adverts.

Leo was rejected for having
a bad haircut.
He was told to change his name
to Lenny Williams.

When Leo was 10
he was sick of being rejected.
His Dad said:
'Just relax.
Some day it will happen for you.'

3 Success

Leo signed with an agent
at the age of 14.
He was in adverts
for toys, bubble gum
and road safety.

Then he got small parts
in TV programmes
like *Lassie* and *Roseanne*.

When he left school at 16,
he didn't go to drama school.
He got his first regular TV part.
He played a homeless boy called Luke
in a teen sitcom
called *Growing Pains*.

This was Leo's first big success.

Leo played Luke in *Growing Pains*.

Life at home
was nothing like the life shown on TV.

His parents were wild
when they were young.
Leo said:
'Whatever I did
would be something
they'd already done.'

So Leo had to rebel
by being sensible.
He said:
'When I wanted a nose ring
Dad said "great",
so I didn't bother.'

Leo was cast in his first film
in 1991.
But he prefers to forget
his part in the cheap horror film
Critters III.

In 1993 he beat 400 other boys
for a part in the film
This Boy's Life.

It was a big break for him.
The film didn't make much money
but it gave Leo's career a boost.

Robert De Niro was the star
but Leo got the best reviews.

With Ellen Barkin and Robert de Niro
in *This Boy's Life*.

Now Leo could choose the films
he wanted to be in.
His Dad helped him choose
which films to star in,
and his Mum
became his manager.

They didn't pick the popular films.
Leo turned down the part of Robin
in *Batman Forever*.
It was his turn to do the rejecting.
He wanted to plan
a long career.

At 6 foot tall
with blonde hair
and blue-green eyes
he has the looks
to play a boy or a man.

4 The Film Star

In 1993 he played Arnie
in *What's Eating Gilbert Grape.*
Arnie is a sloppy, cheerful boy
who has learning difficulties.

Again, the 19 year old Leo
walked off with the best reviews.
He was nominated for an Oscar.
He was glad not to win
because he was scared
of making a speech.

His next part was in a Western
with Sharon Stone in 1995.
She wanted him
to be in the film so much
that she paid his wage
out of her own.

In the same year
he made two more films
playing very serious parts.

In *The Basketball Diaries*
he played a young basketball star
who turns to a life
of drugs and crime.
The critics said
his acting was brilliant.

Next Leo played a gay French poet
in the film *Total Eclipse*.
The public didn't like the film.
At the same time,
the papers were full of stories
of his drinking and fighting.
The hot young star was falling.
How could he save his career?

Leo in *Basketball Diaries*.

In less than a year Leo was back.
He played Romeo
in a modern film version of
Romeo and Juliet.
It was set in a fantasy world.
The story took place
on Verona Beach, USA.

The film was a success
and Leo was a success.
It made him one of
the most sought-after Hollywood actors
for the first time in his career.

With Clare Danes in *Romeo and Juliet*.

In the same year, 1996,
he starred with Robert De Niro again.
The film was called *Marvin's Room*.

Leo played the part
of a disturbed boy
who sets fire to his mother's house.

Now Leo had the money he needed
to buy a house.
He moved into
a six-bedroomed house
in Hollywood.

There he keeps his silver BMW
and his many pairs
of cheap sunglasses
that he buys on his travels.

5 Titanic

Leo has often said
that if he didn't make a success
of acting
he would study the ocean.

He spends a lot of time by the ocean
and in it, swimming and diving.
He has a scar on his arm
from a jellyfish sting.

Leo's next film, in 1996,
was set on the ocean.
It was based on
the true story
of the tragic sinking of the Titanic
on its first ocean trip.

1,523 people died
when the Titanic sank in 1912.
The writers added to this true story
the love story
of a poor boy (played by Leo)
and a rich girl.

People have said
that it's Romeo and Juliet
on the ocean.

At first
Leo didn't want to make the film.
It had a big budget
and this scared Leo.
The film had to make $200 million
to cover its costs.
Some said it was impossible.

Leo and Kate Winslet in *Titanic*.

Titanic was a difficult film to make.
It had breath-taking special effects.
It took nearly a year to make,
with long hours
and lots of upsets.
Leo said this comes with the job.

Titanic turned out to be
a blockbuster.
It has broken all box office records
and it won 11 Oscars.

This time Leo was not nominated
and his fans said it wasn't fair.

As soon as *Titanic* was finished,
Leo went to France
to make *The Man In The Iron Mask*.

This is the story
of identical twins
and Leo plays both of them.

One twin is the King of France,
Louis XIV.
The other twin is kept in prison
in an iron mask.

The King is not popular.
So the three musketeers
plan to swap over the two brothers
and save France.
It's a swash-buckling action story.

Leo played the King of France
in *The Man In The Iron Mask*.

Leo is the only US actor in history
to be in two top films
at the same time.

There are reports
that he can ask $20 million
for his next film.

Leo-mania is sweeping the world.
Fans follow him everywhere.
He has no plans to make another film
for a year.

He says: 'I'm now taking a year off
because I want to slow down.
I just feel there are other things
I need to do.'

Maybe he'll travel
and go back to his roots
in that small town in Italy.